MW00331381

Hooked on Fly Fishing from A to Z

Hooked
on
Fly Fishing
from
A to Z

Beverly Vidrine

Illustrated by:
Matthew Tabbert

Copyright © 2013
By Beverly Vidrine

Illustrations Copyright © 2013
Matthew Tabbert
All Rights Reserved

For my husband, Dennis,
who hooked me into fly fishing.
BV

Acknowledgement:
A special thanks to Dave Hughes for reading my manuscript.

Cover and book designed by Wayne C. Parmley
All text for this book is set in ITC Novarese

ISBN: 0-9788009-4-X

Printed in the United States of America
Published by: Beverly Vidrine, Lafayette, LA

Introduction

Did you know that long before Christ was born fishermen watched fish eat a kind of insect that floated on the water? Instead of catching the insect to use as bait, they tied wool and feathers around a hook to look like the real bug. Then they used a rod and line to throw this artificial fly to the water. When the fish opened its mouth to eat the fly, it was caught by the fishhook. Today, there are new kinds of rods, lines, and flies. The adventure of fly fishing has become fun and exciting.

Angler

If you are hooked on fishing, you're an angler. An angler catches game fish with a rod and reel. If you use bait you are bait fishing, but if you cast with an artificial fly, you are fly fishing. Either way, wade in the water, stand on the shore or on a pier, or go get the fish by fishing from a boat.

Adams

The word "angle" comes from a very old word "anke," which means fishing with an angle or bend like the fishhook you use now.

Boat

Travel on different kinds of water in a vessel or boat, a canoe, a row boat, or even an outboard motor boat. Now and then, you fish from a belly boat or a flats boat or the top of a kayak.

No matter what kind of boat you use, move about quietly since any noise spooks the fish.

Black Beetle

Cast of the Fly

You should have lessons from fly fishers on how to cast or throw the artificial fly. At the start, pull some line off the reel, then grip the cork handle. Move the rod backward and forward toward the fishing spot. Let the heavy line unroll into a loop to deliver the light fly to the water. Watch the fly drift on or in the water and hope that it will attract a fish.

Caterpillar

Bait or spin fishing is different - the heavy lure pulls the line out.

Dry Fly

A dry fly or floating fly will float on the water to hook a fish that feeds there. After casting, keep an eye on it as it glides on top of the water. It looks almost like an ant or dragonfly that fell on the water, drifts downstream, and seems like food to a fish. Watch the fish rise to take the fly.

Tie a dry fly by wrapping rooster feathers, or deer hair, or other materials that float, around a hook to make it look like a real insect.

Dragon Fly

Eddy

When fishing, look for water traveling in a circle near logs, boulders, or the shore. This eddy happens in rivers and streams where fast-moving water meets slow-moving water. Land insects that fall from trees and bushes, like caterpillars, beetles, and inchworms, get caught in the eddy. Watch for fish that usually swim the slow water searching the eddy for food.

Elk Hair Caddis

Maybe the fish see the eddy as a fast-food restaurant.

Fly-fishing

Get serious about being a fly fisher. Dress a hook with fur and feathers to make a fly so that it looks like food fish want to eat. When ready to fly fish, cast the heavy fly line just right, and the light fly will attract the fish. As soon as you catch a fish, bring it in and take a picture.

Frog

You can return the fish to the water to help keep the waters full of fish. That's called "Catch and Release"!

Gear

Wear special clothes to walk or wade through streams. Choose colors that blend well with the water and trees, so the fish won't see you. Wrap a belt around your chest waders and snap the suspenders to protect you from the cold water. Wear comfy clothes underneath and well-fitted wading socks and shoes. Include your sunglasses and a fly-fishing vest.

Gray Ghost

For safety, hold on to a wading staff to prevent a fall on slippery rocks in cold, deep waters.

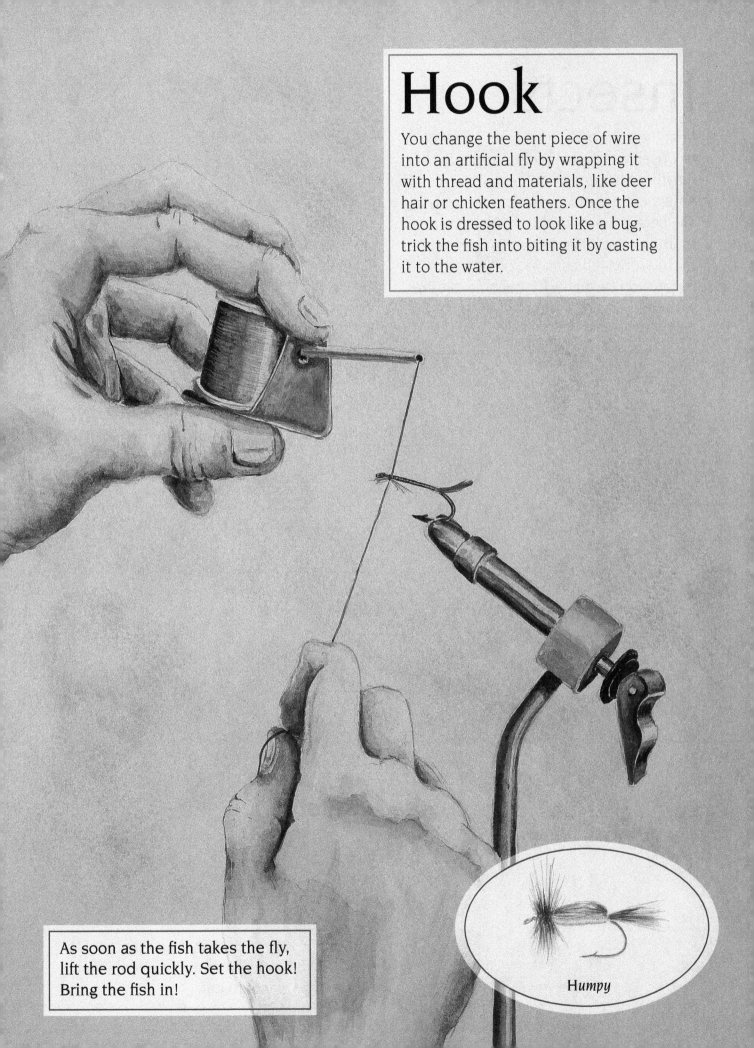

Hook

You change the bent piece of wire into an artificial fly by wrapping it with thread and materials, like deer hair or chicken feathers. Once the hook is dressed to look like a bug, trick the fish into biting it by casting it to the water.

As soon as the fish takes the fly, lift the rod quickly. Set the hook! Bring the fish in!

Humpy

Insects

Imagine swimming quietly underwater to observe the aquatic flies and bugs like mayflies and stoneflies. Terrestrial flies like ants, beetles, and grasshoppers are easy to see because they live on land and often fall on the water. Since fish eat these insects, make artificial flies to look like them. Before you tie a fake fly, become familiar with the parts of an insect: tail, body, legs, and wings.

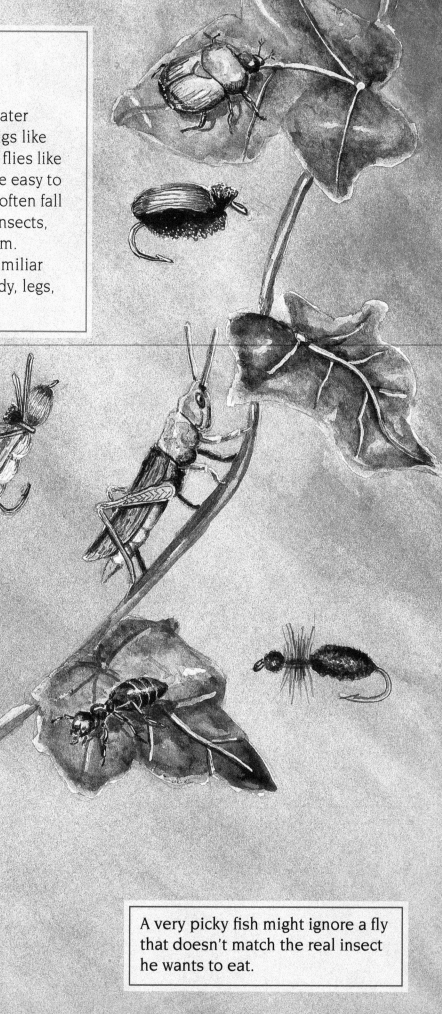

Ida May

A very picky fish might ignore a fly that doesn't match the real insect he wants to eat.

Jumping Fish

Fish out of water! Meet the incredible Rainbow Trout known for its jumping ability. The strong Rainbow fights hard when hooked, leaping out of the water over and over again.

Fish for Rainbow Trout in cool, clear streams, lakes and rivers.

Joe's Hopper

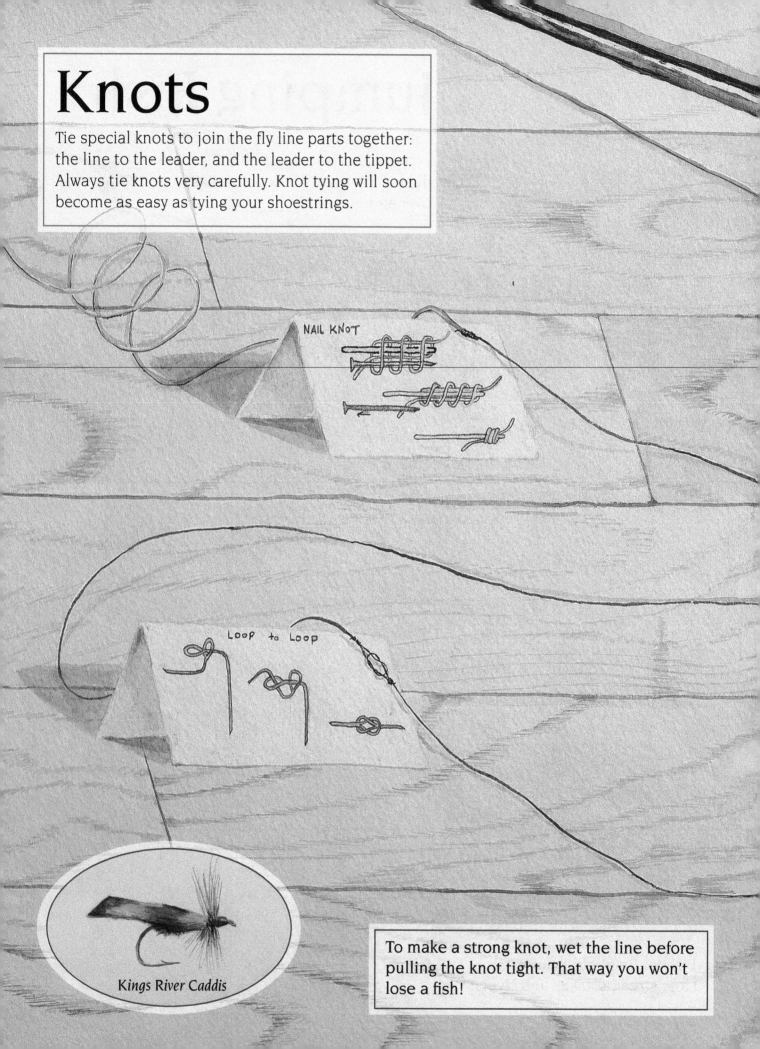

Knots

Tie special knots to join the fly line parts together: the line to the leader, and the leader to the tippet. Always tie knots very carefully. Knot tying will soon become as easy as tying your shoestrings.

NAIL KNOT

LOOP to LOOP

Kings River Caddis

To make a strong knot, wet the line before pulling the knot tight. That way you won't lose a fish!

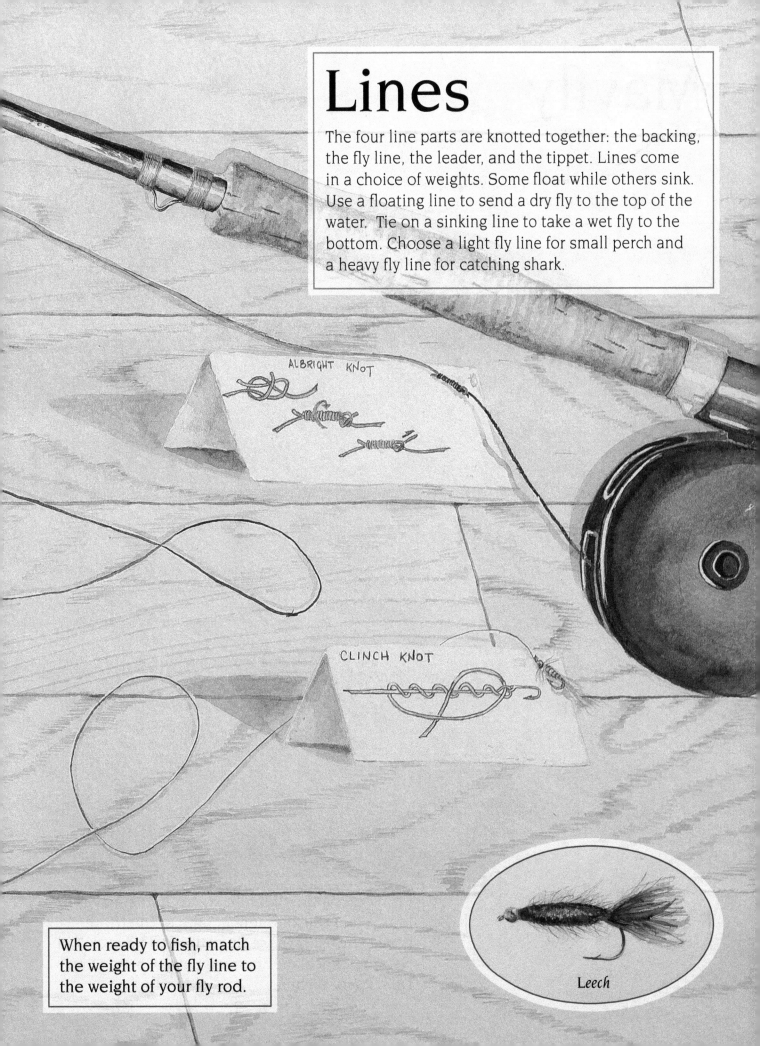

Lines

The four line parts are knotted together: the backing, the fly line, the leader, and the tippet. Lines come in a choice of weights. Some float while others sink. Use a floating line to send a dry fly to the top of the water. Tie on a sinking line to take a wet fly to the bottom. Choose a light fly line for small perch and a heavy fly line for catching shark.

ALBRIGHT KNOT

CLINCH KNOT

When ready to fish, match the weight of the fly line to the weight of your fly rod.

Leech

Mayfly

Discover the long-tailed insect that fish like to eat. The Mayfly hatches underwater and grows into a tiny bug that swims then crawls out of the water, and soon flies away.

March Brown

Fish feed on the different stages in the mayfly's life cycle. Fly fishermen imitate, or "match the hatch," by using these fly patterns: Pheasant Tail Nymph, Chocolate Emerger, Blue-Winged Olive Dun, Rusty Spinner.

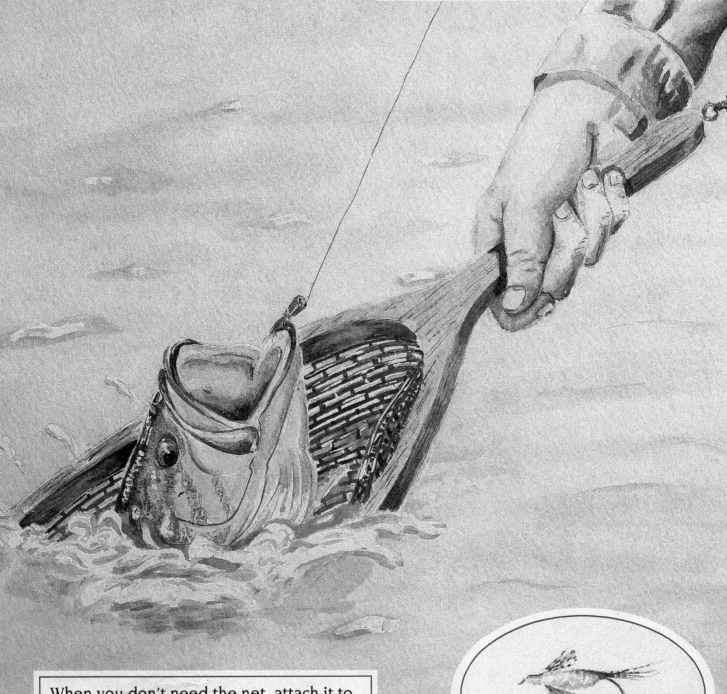

Net

You land fish quickly by using a landing net. Lead the fish, without chasing it, into this mesh bag. Once it is in the net, take a picture of your catch, and let it go.

When you don't need the net, attach it to the D-ring on the back of your fishing vest. Then it is out of your way and within easy reach when you need it.

Near Enough

Outdoors

Fly fishing brings you outside to lakes and ponds where you catch fish or simply enjoy some quiet time in the warm sun. At the same time you're having fun and making memories of the wildlife you see in a country setting.

Olive Scud

While out there try flipping rocks to find insects and you'll know what the fish are eating.

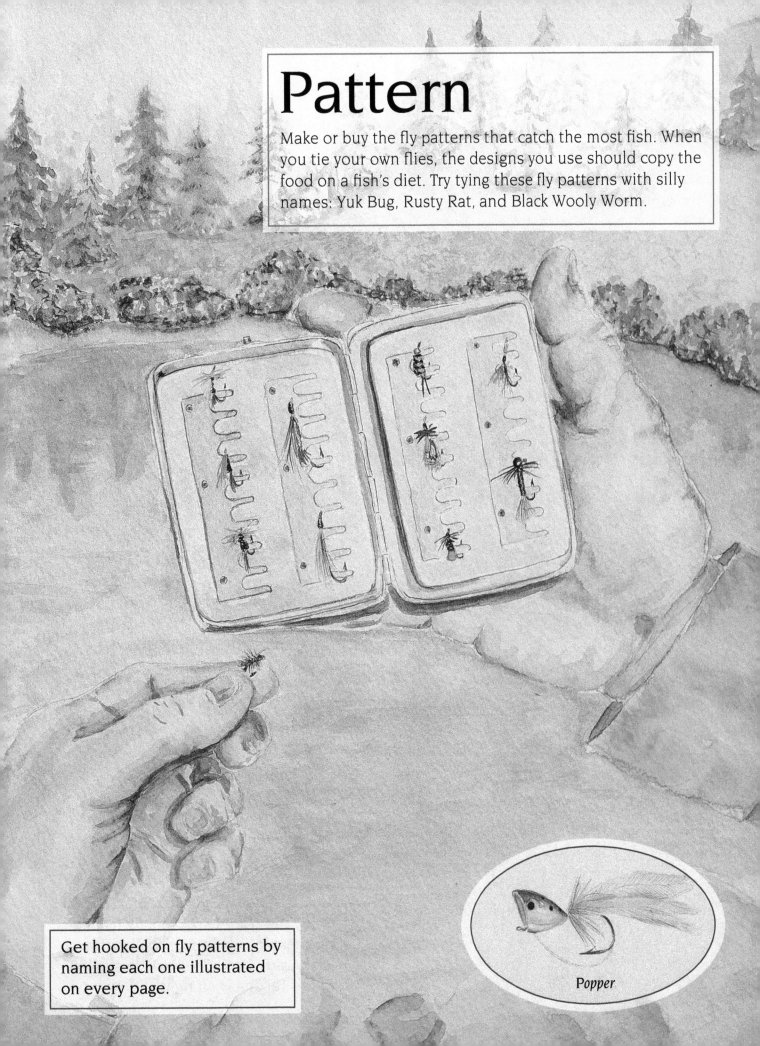

Pattern

Make or buy the fly patterns that catch the most fish. When you tie your own flies, the designs you use should copy the food on a fish's diet. Try tying these fly patterns with silly names: Yuk Bug, Rusty Rat, and Black Wooly Worm.

Get hooked on fly patterns by naming each one illustrated on every page.

Popper

Quarry

Search the waters for fish. Since fish find food near their cover, learn where they hide. Find your quarry in water hiding near weeds, near rocks, near fallen trees, and behind boulders on the bottom.

Quill Gordon

Enjoy the "quiet sport" of fly fishing by sneaking up on fish. Walk softly on a lake side or wade slowly in shallow water. Talking is all right!

Rod & Reel

Your fly rod acts as a tool for casting line and controlling fish. It has a cork handle to grip with your casting hand, a reel seat to hold the reel, and guides for the line. You'll find a hook keeper near the handle. The fly reel stores line and provides drag to land fast or heavy fish.

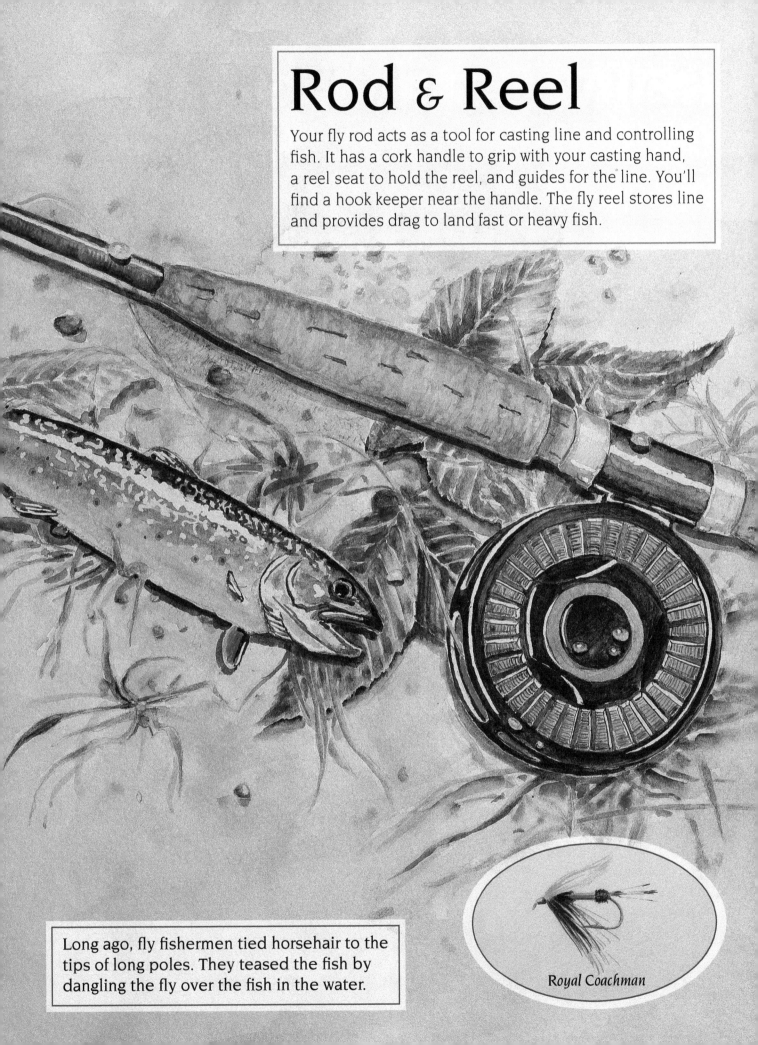

Long ago, fly fishermen tied horsehair to the tips of long poles. They teased the fish by dangling the fly over the fish in the water.

Royal Coachman

Saltwater Fly Fishing

Fly Fish the salty oceans to find saltwater fish. You'll find saltwater fly fishing different from freshwater fishing in lakes, streams, and ponds. Ocean fish swim faster, are stronger, and eat larger things, so the tackle is big and heavy.

Snapping Shrimp

The hooks used in saltwater are made of stainless steel to keep from rusting.

Tackle

Fly fishing tackle includes a rod, a reel, a line, a leader, and a fly. Use this same outfit to catch trout in rivers, bass in lakes, and bluegills in ponds.

Timberline

Fly anglers use many tools and gadgets to prepare and keep up their tackle.

Underwater Hideout

Since fish don't have eyelids they usually stay away from the sun light and look for cover. They hide and feed in shade provided by logs, rocks, and other underwater stuff. Don't forget to look for some of these places when you fly fish!

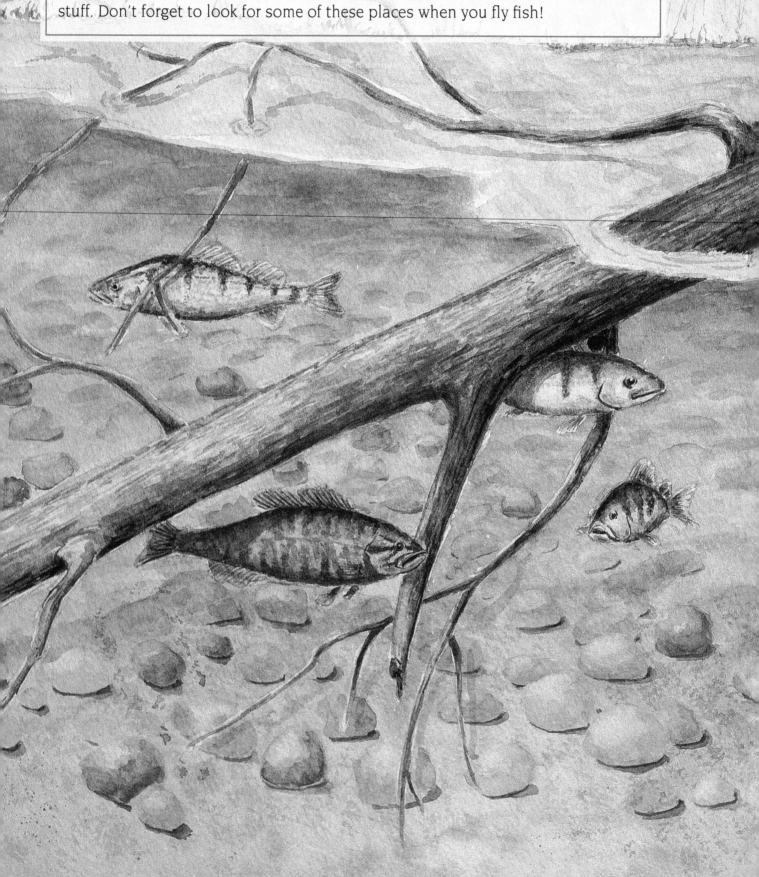

Do you know any fishermen who throw old Christmas trees in lakes or ponds to help fish find a safe underwater hideout?

Ugly bug

Vest

Your fly fishing vest includes pockets on the outside and inside to store gear such as fly boxes for flies, clippers for cutting line, forceps for removing the hook, fly line and leader for extra supplies, and maybe a sandwich for lunch.

Vance's Critter

Use the rod holder on your vest to free your hands for tying flies and knots.

Wet Fly

You tie a wet fly to sink underwater. Since fish feed on the bottom tie on a wet fly to catch fish there. Cast the wet fly across a stream, watch it swing with the moving water, and then disappear underneath.

Woolly Bugger

A curious fish might see your wet fly as a drowning insect.

X-size

The letter X plus a number represents the thickness and strength of the leader and tippet. Arranged from 0X to 8X, a thick leader and tippet have a low X number, and a thin leader and tippet have a high X number.

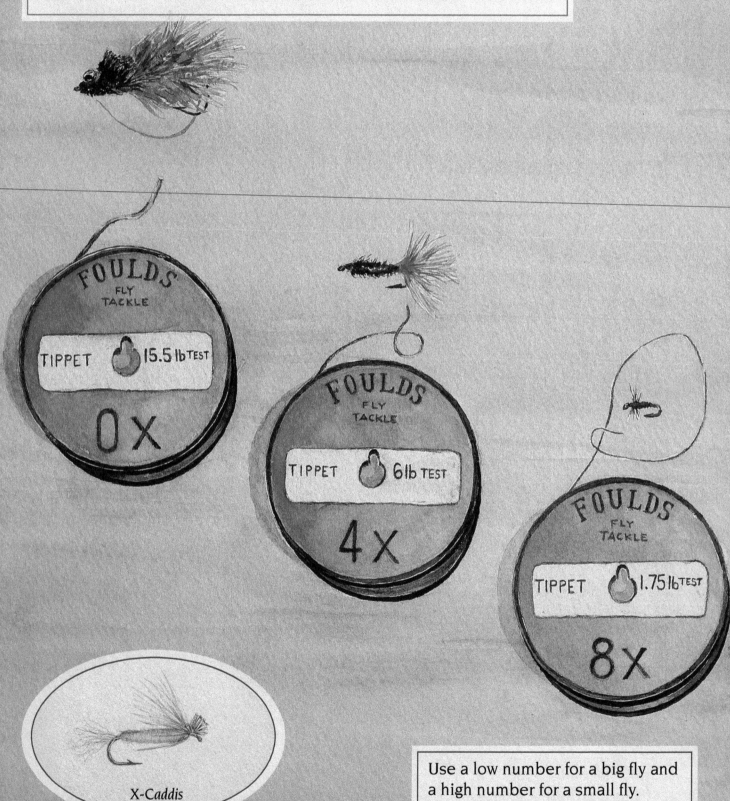

FOULDS
FLY TACKLE

TIPPET 15.5 lb TEST

0X

FOULDS
FLY TACKLE

TIPPET 6 lb TEST

4X

FOULDS
FLY TACKLE

TIPPET 1.75 lb TEST

8X

X-Caddis

Use a low number for a big fly and a high number for a small fly.

Yarn Fly

You can use a yarn fly to practice fly casting in a safe way. Just tie a piece of yarn about one inch long to the end of your leader. Set up a practice field by laying hula hoops down in the yard. Cast your line and try to place the yarn fly inside the hoops.

Shield your eyes by wearing sunglasses anytime you are casting.

Yuk Bug

Zinger

Pin a retracting zinger on your vest to hold clippers. Pull the clippers down, clip the line, and let it go. The zinger cord pulls the clippers right back until you need them again. Buy another zinger to hold other tools like pliers or a hook sharpener.

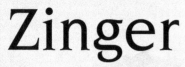

Zug Bug

Give fish a chance to stay alive after a catch. Wet your hands, and hold the fish upside down carefully. Remove the hook. Hold the fish upright underwater, release it and let it swim away.

CPSIA information can be obtained
at www.ICGtesting.com
Printed in the USA
LVHW020855220723
752809LV00031B/287

9 780978 800949